# the Healthy Family
# slow cooker
## COOKBOOK

# the Healthy Family slow cooker
## COOKBOOK

## CHRISTINA DYMOCK

FRONT TABLE BOOKS
AN IMPRINT OF CEDAR FORT, INC. | SPRINGVILLE, UTAH

ISBN 13: 978-1-4621-1625-6

Published by Front Table Books, an imprint of Cedar Fort, Inc.
2373 W. 700 S., Springville, UT 84663
Distributed by Cedar Fort, Inc., www.cedarfort.com

Library of Congress Cataloging-in-Publication data on file.

Cover and page design by M. Shaun McMurdie
Cover design © 2015 by Lyle Mortimer
Edited by Deborah Spencer

Printed in China

10 9 8 7 6 5 4 3 2 1

Printed on acid-free paper

# TO MOM

Who made me take my vitamins and eat my veggies.

Love you!

# Also by Christina Dymock:

*The Hungry Family Slow Cooker Cookbook*

*The Bacon Lover's Cookbook*

*Young Chefs: Cooking Skills and Recipes for Kids*

*One Dirty Bowl: Fast Desserts, Faster Cleanup*

# CONTENTS

## Welcome to The Healthy Family Slow Cooker Cookbook

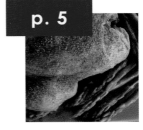

**Poultry**

**Pork**

**Beef**

**Soup & Salad**

**Sides**

**Sweet Endings**

## WELCOME TO

# the Healthy Family
# slow cooker
## COOKBOOK

## Health Benefits of Slow Cooking

Each family has their own set of eating habits. In order to improve the quality of their meals, they may need to cut back on carbs or sugar; or they might need to eat gluten-free for medical purposes. Whatever your family's needs are, you'll find delicious recipes in this book to help your family eat better.

Slow cooking is the perfect way to make healthy meals for your family because it doesn't require a lot of time. In light of the fact that parents are super busy, I've created recipes that come together with little preparation and provide lots of flavor. The down-home selections in this book are fast, healthy, and delicious. There's no frilly ingredients or complicated steps. It's just yummy food that's good for you.

Instead of trying to overhaul your family's unhealthy eating habits all at once, try easing them into new flavors and patterns. There are several ideas listed below. Pick one to work on and once it becomes a habit, try another.

## Look for Sugar-Free Products

Sugar is a preservative that is used in almost all prepackaged foods. Because it's practically omnipresent, a lot of the sugar in our diets sneaks in under the radar. Take some time to read packaging and become conscious of the ingredients. Even switching out a few products for the sugar-free counterpart will improve your family's health. The Sweet Endings section of this book has many sugar-free options for desserts that your family is sure to enjoy. You may not feel the need to ban all sugar from your home, just be aware of how it's getting in.

## Buy Low/Lower Sodium Products

Like sugar, salt is a preservative for canned or processed food. However, many people add additional salt when they cook with or serve pre-prepared meals. A good rule of thumb is to buy the low/lower sodium product and add salt to taste.

## Use Fresh or Frozen Vegetables and Fruits

Fresh veggies are chock-full of the nutrients that make them so good for you and your family. Frozen fruits and veggies are picked when ripe and kept from decaying through the freezing process. If you can't get fresh, frozen is best.

## Switch to Whole Grains

Kids (and husbands) may balk when they see whole grain breads on the table, but they'll get used to it soon enough. Start out with breads or rolls that don't have seeds or grains on top. Children are sensitive to textures. Instead, look for plain wheat bread and try serving it spread with sugar-free jam or a little honey. Once they realize it's not evil, they'll be open to trying new breads with grains and seeds. Don't stop at rolls and breads. Keep an eye out for cereals, tortillas, and crackers made with whole grains too.

## Have a Family Meal

Studies show that families that eat at least one meal together have healthier eating habits. A family meal can help strengthen the bonds between siblings, provide a way for family members to de-stress, and help picky eaters make healthy food choices. With so many benefits, it's worth the effort to get everyone together for dinner. With a slow cooker, it's easy to provide hearty food that tastes good.

## Making a Slow Cooker Friend

Once you start using a slow cooker, you'll find out how addicting it is to set up the slow cooker, run through your day, and come home to a marvelous meal. Your slow cooker will become your new BCF (best cooking friend.)

## Which Slow Cooker Should You Buy?

There are dozens of models of slow cookers out there. Some can even work as a skillet before they switch to slow cooking. That's advantageous for recipes that require you to brown meat before adding it to the slow cooker. While I try to be conscious when planning meals, there always seems to be a day or two where I scramble because I forgot to thaw the ground beef or turkey. On those days, I follow the method found on page 74 for browning meat in the slow cooker and I'm back on track.

It doesn't matter what brand or model of slow cooker you purchase. They are all built to do the same thing: slow cook. (Big surprise, I know.) If you're just starting out, buy the basic model. If you want an upgrade, feel free. I find that it's extremely easy to justify a new slow cooker. In fact, I bought two new ones just to write this book. One was the largest size available, used to make whole chickens with veggies. The other was a smaller one I could use for sides and desserts.

If you have a large family, buy a large slow cooker. There's no point in making a meal that will only feed half of you. Also, if you plan on cooking whole chickens, like the one on page 19, you'll want an oval-shaped slow cooker. They will fit the bird and still have space for veggies. Even when my family was younger, I cooked whole birds and used the leftovers for soups, enchiladas, or salads. A whole bird will provide chicken stock that's much better than the store-bought stuff too.

## Getting to Know Your New Friend

Take some time to get to know your slow cooker. Some brands take longer to heat up or cook at a lower, though still safe, temperature that will increase your cook time.

Before you can count on your slow cooker, you need to understand its personality. For your first meal, cook a recipe you're familiar with. Check it one hour earlier than you normally would to gauge cook time. *But* plan at least an hour extra in case the slow cooker takes longer than anticipated.

If you are new to the world of slow cooking, use the recipe as a gauge for your new slow cooker. In general, slow cooker recipes have a range of cooking time. The recipe will say something like, "cook for 6–8 hours on low." During the honeymoon phase of owning a slow cooker, check the food at the earliest time. You can insert a thermometer into the meat, use a fork to test the veggies and see if they are tender, or test the cake with a toothpick. If it needs to cook longer, replace the lid and wait 30 minutes to an hour before testing again. Once you and your slow cooker develop an understanding, it will become second nature to judge cooking times.

# Basic Slow Cooker Care

I killed one of my slow cookers not too long ago. It was an accident, I promise. I dropped it and it shattered. So sad. Thankfully, it was empty so I didn't end up with dinner all over the floor. Needless to say, slow cookers are more fragile than they appear. Here's a few tips for keeping your slow cooker in tip-top condition.

1. **Don't drop it.**

2. **Use soft cloths for cleaning.** The finish on a slow cooker liner can be scratched. Use warm water and liquid dish soap to clean the liner, or place it in the dishwasher. Being dishwasher-safe is one of the benefits of slow cookers with removable liners.

3. **Always let your slow cooker cool before washing.** The ceramic liner cannot handle drastic changes in temperature. If you want to speed up the cooling process, remove the liner from the heating unit and dump out the contents. Once it's cool, use warm, but not hot, water to wash or soak the liner.

4. **To clean the heating unit,** use a mild cleaner and a soft cloth. Please make sure you unplug the slow cooker before cleaning and never submerse the heating unit in water!

5. **The slow cooker liner will retain heat,** even when removed from the heating base, which makes it perfect as a serving dish. Be sure to use a trivet since the bottom of the liner will scorch a table or countertop.

6. **Because it retains heat,** it is not recommended that you store food in the slow cooker. It's better to remove the leftovers and store them in an air-tight container in the fridge as soon as possible.

# Poultry

# Sunday Turkey Roast and Broccoli

| Serves 8 | 4–6 hours on high or 6–8 hours on low |
|---|---|

1 (4- to 5-lb.) turkey breast

3 tsp. reduced sodium chicken bouillon

½ cup hot water

1 tsp. onion powder

½ tsp. parsley

½ tsp. celery seed

¼ tsp. paprika

¼ tsp. black pepper

4 cups chopped broccoli

Sundays are traditionally a "big dinner" day. But I don't want to spend my Sunday in the kitchen. With this recipe, we can still enjoy a special Sunday meal without all the stress.

## directions

**PLACE THE TURKEY BREAST** in a large slow cooker. Dissolve the bouillon in the water and pour over the turkey. Sprinkle the onion powder, parsley, celery seed, paprika, and black pepper over the turkey. Cover and cook on low for 6–8 hours or on high for 4–6 hours. Add the broccoli for the last 30 minutes of cooking.

# Chicken and Asparagus Dinner

| Serves 8 | 7-9½ hours on low, total |
|---|---|

1 (3.5- to 4.5-lb.) whole chicken with the innards removed

1 (14.4-oz.) can low sodium chicken broth

1 tsp. paprika

½ tsp. pepper

2 tsp. garlic powder

1 tsp. onion powder

1 tsp. basil

1 bunch asparagus

*If you buy your asparagus in advance, place the bottoms in a cup of water and store it in the fridge to help keep it fresh.*

## directions

**PLACE THE CHICKEN** in the slow cooker. Pour the chicken broth over the chicken. In a small bowl, mix together the paprika, pepper, garlic powder, onion powder, and basil. Sprinkle over the chicken. Cover and cook on low for 6–8 hours. Wash the asparagus and trim off the bottoms. Lay asparagus over chicken. Cover and cook for the last 60–90 minutes of cooking time, or until the asparagus is cooked through.

Christina Dymock

# Turkey Veggie Sloppy Joe

| Serves 6 | 4–6 hours on low |
|---|---|

1 lb. ground turkey

2 celery ribs, chopped

1 green or yellow pepper, chopped

½ cup chopped broccoli or cauliflower

½ cup chopped carrots

1 green onion, chopped

1 Tbsp. honey

2 Tbsp. balsamic vinegar

1 tsp. cilantro

3 Tbsp. no-salt-added tomato sauce

6 crusty wheat rolls

Sloppy joes are a mainstay in big families. Here's a healthier version. I hope your family enjoys it as much as mine. Feel free to throw in your own favorite veggies.

## directions

**REMOVE THE TURKEY** from the package and place in the slow cooker. Do not break it into small pieces. Add the celery, pepper, broccoli or cauliflower, carrots, onion, honey, vinegar, and cilantro to the slow cooker. Cook on low for 4–6 hours. Remove the turkey. It will be in the shape of a loaf. Cut it into ¼-inch pieces. Return the meat to the slow cooker and add the tomato sauce. Stir the sauce, meat, and veggies together. Cut the rolls in half and fill with meat sauce. Top with additional veggies if desired and serve.

# Turkey Loaf

| Serves 8 | 4 hours on high |
|---|---|

2 lb. ground turkey

⅓ cup fresh parsley

2 cloves garlic, minced

¼ cup chopped onion

1½ cups crushed low sodium saltine crackers

2 eggs

*D*on't let the simple preparation fool you—this dinner packs a hearty punch. Because the meat is slow cooked, it comes out especially tender. Even young kids, who sometimes have a hard time with meat loaf, eat this up!

## directions

**SPRAY A SLOW COOKER** with nonstick cooking spray and set aside. Combine all ingredients in a medium-sized mixing bowl. Transfer to the prepared slow cooker and spread evenly. Cover and cook on high for 4 hours.

Christina Dymock

# Bacon-Wrapped Chicken Fingers

| Serves 6 | 2½–3½ hours on low, total |
|----------|---------------------------|

½ cup whole wheat flour

1½ tsp. rosemary

½ tsp. garlic powder

¼ tsp. pepper

½ tsp. oregano

2 lb. chicken fingers

1 (16-oz.) pkg. low sodium turkey bacon

*K*ids love foods they can eat with their hands, and these bacon-wrapped chicken fingers are perfect. Be sure to let them cool before handing over to little fingers.

## directions

**ON A FLAT PLATE,** combine the flour, rosemary, garlic powder, pepper, and oregano. Take one chicken finger and rinse it under cold water. Roll it in the flour mixture and then wrap it in bacon. It may take two pieces of bacon to go the length of the chicken. Secure the bacon with toothpicks. Place the chicken in the bottom of a slow cooker. Repeat with remaining chicken and bacon. Cover and cook on low for 2–3 hours or until the chicken is cooked through. Tip the lid of the slow cooker to allow moisture to escape and cook an additional 30 minutes.

# Sun-Dried Tomato Turkey Roast

| Serves 8 | 6–8 hours on low |
|----------|------------------|

1 (3- to 4-lb.) turkey breast

½ onion, sliced

2 Tbsp. lemon juice

¼ tsp. paprika

1 Tbsp. oregano

½ cup fat-free, low sodium chicken broth

½ cup drained and julienne-cut sun-dried tomatoes

Sun-dried tomatoes are the best tomatoes in the world! They have the perfect flavor to add to everything from pizza to spaghetti sauce. It's perfectly acceptable to hoard them for yourself and smother your serving, but be ready to share because they are sooooo good.

## directions

**PLACE THE TURKEY BREAST** in the slow cooker. Spread the onions over and around the turkey. Sprinkle turkey with lemon juice, paprika, and oregano. Pour the chicken broth down the side of the slow cooker. Place the sun-dried tomatoes on top of the breast. Cover and cook on low for 6–8 hours, or until cooked through.

Christina Dymock

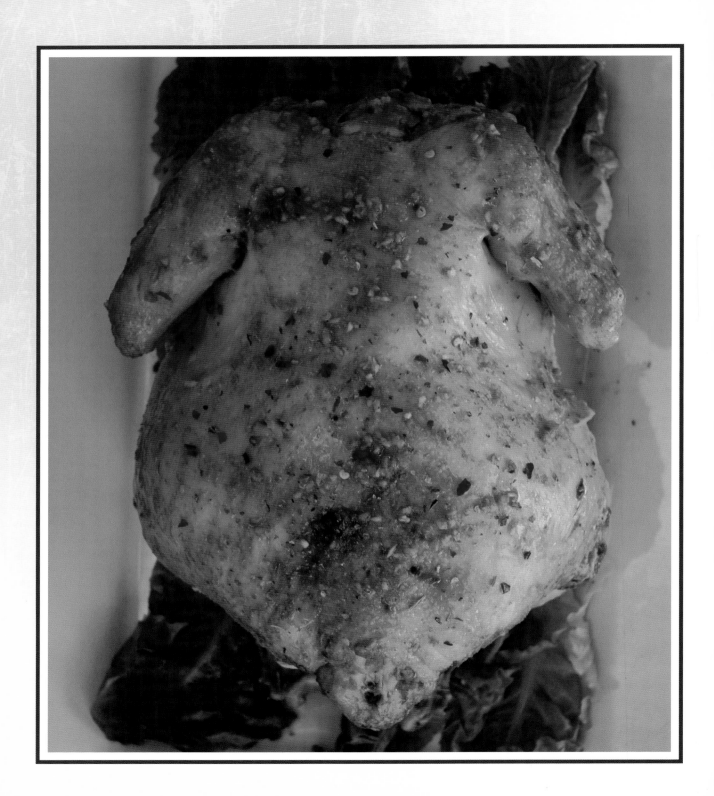

# Company Chicken

| Serves 8 | 6-8 hours on low |
|----------|------------------|

1 (4- to 5-lb.) whole chicken
1 Tbsp. olive oil
2 tsp. spicy mustard
2 tsp. paprika
1½ tsp. onion powder
2 cloves garlic, minced
1½ tsp. basil
1 tsp. cumin
½ tsp. pepper
½ tsp. thyme

*I love cooking whole chickens. Not only do I get to keep the chicken stock for use in other recipes, I usually have enough chicken left over for lunch the next day. If there is enough leftovers, I will use it to make the tamales found on page 36.*

## directions

**PLACE THE CHICKEN** in a large slow cooker. In a small bowl, whisk together the olive oil, mustard, paprika, onion powder, garlic, basil, cumin, pepper, and thyme. Brush the spices over the chicken. Cover and cook on low for 6–8 hours, or until the chicken is cooked through.

# Chicken Gyros

| Serves 6 | 4–6 hours on high or 6–8 hours on low |
|---|---|

3 lb. boneless chicken breasts

2 Tbsp. olive oil

1 tsp. cumin

1 tsp. paprika

1 tsp. oregano

1 tsp. rosemary

1 clove garlic, minced

1 red onion

6 slices of flat bread

**Tzatziki Sauce**

½ cup plain Greek yogurt

2 Tbsp. lemon juice

1 tsp. dill

¼ tsp. pepper

1 cucumber

*There are some meals that lend themselves to being served buffet style. This is one of those meals. Place all the fillings on the table and let everyone build their own gyro. That way everyone gets what they want!*

## directions

**CUT THE CHICKEN** into strips and place in a large zip-top bag. Add the olive oil, cumin, paprika, oregano, rosemary, and garlic to the bag. Allow the mix to marinate in the fridge for 4 hours or overnight. Place the chicken in the slow cooker and cook on low for 6–8 hours or on high for 4–6 hours, or until the chicken is cooked through.

**TZATZIKI SAUCE:** Place the yogurt in a small bowl. Add the lemon juice, dill, and pepper. Peel and chop the cucumber and add it to the sauce. Stir well.

**TO SERVE:** Cut the onion into thin strips. Make gyros by placing chicken on the flat bread, covering it in sauce, and then adding a hearty layer of onions. Wrap the bread and serve.

Christina Dymock

# Chicken Quesadillas

**Serves 6** | **2–3 hours on high or 3–4 hours on low**

- 2 cups cooked and chopped chicken
- 1 yellow pepper, chopped
- 1 green pepper, chopped
- 1 Roma tomato, chopped
- 1 red onion, chopped
- 1 (2.25-oz.) can sliced olives
- 1 (15.25-oz.) can no-salt-added black beans, rinsed
- 1 heaping Tbsp. mild diced chilies
- 1/3 cup light Miracle Whip
- 4 whole wheat tortillas
- 2 Tbsp. water
- shredded cheddar cheese and low-fat sour cream for topping

*There are two ways to serve this dish. The first is to just scoop it out of the slow cooker. The second is to invert the slow cooker onto a serving dish. Lift and present the stack of quesadillas. I recommend practicing the second technique—it took me a couple tries to get it right. No one complained though.*

## directions

**IN A MEDIUM-SIZED BOWL,** combine the chicken, peppers, tomato, onion, olives, black beans, chilies, and Miracle Whip. Spray a large slow cooker with nonstick cooking spray. Place ¼ of the chicken mixture in the slow cooker and cover with a tortilla. Repeat three times with remaining chicken mixture and tortillas. Pour the water down the sides of the slow cooker. Cover and cook on low for 3–4 hours or on high for 2–3 hours. Slice and top with shredded cheddar cheese and sour cream if desired.

# Hot Chicken Sandwiches

| Serves 6 | 6–8 hours on low |
|----------|------------------|

3 chicken breasts
1 tsp. smoky paprika
¼ tsp. chili powder
3 green onions, chopped
1 red pepper, chopped
12 slices of whole wheat
    bread

*These sandwiches are hot in two ways; they are spicy and served warm. You can top them with cheese if you like, but we prefer them plain.*

## directions

**PLACE THE CHICKEN** in a large slow cooker. Sprinkle with paprika and chili powder. Place the onions and red pepper around and on top of the chicken. Cover and cook on low for 6–8 hours, or until the chicken shreds easily. Shred the chicken and serve on whole wheat bread.

# Marinated Drumsticks

| Serves 8 | 4-6 hours on high or 6-8 hours on low |
|---|---|

- 1½ cups "less sodium" soy sauce
- ½ cup water
- 1 tsp. reduced sodium chicken bouillon granules
- 2 Tbsp. canola oil
- 2 Tbsp. Worcestershire sauce
- 5 cloves garlic, minced
- 2 tsp. freshly grated ginger
- 2 Tbsp. honey
- 16 chicken drumsticks

You can cook this recipe without marinating the chicken first, but it's so much better when it has time to absorb all the flavors. If you're in a hurry, feel free to just throw it all in the slow cooker.

## directions

**IN A MEDIUM-SIZED BOWL,** mix together the soy sauce, water, bouillon, canola oil, Worcestershire sauce, garlic, ginger, and honey. Reserve 1 cup of the marinade and place in the refrigerator. Place the chicken in a zip-top bag. Pour the remaining marinade over the chicken, seal the bag, and allow to marinate for 6 hours or overnight.

**DRAIN** the marinade sauce off the chicken. Place the chicken in a large slow cooker and pour the reserved marinade over the chicken. Cover and cook on low for 6–8 hours or on high for 4–6 hours, or until chicken is cooked through.

# Chicken and Artichoke Fettuccini

| Serves 8 | 4–6 hours on low, total |
|---|---|

2 lb. boneless chicken thighs

1 (13.75-oz.) can artichoke hearts

3 cloves garlic, minced

1 tsp. basil

¼ tsp. thyme

2 oz. cream cheese

¼ cup cream

1 cup water

2 Tbsp. flour

1 (16-oz.) pkg. pasta

round here, the thicker the alfredo sauce, the better. If your family likes the sauce thinner, all you need to do is omit some or all of the flour.

## directions

**PLACE THE CHICKEN** in a large slow cooker. Cover and cook on low for 2–4 hours or until the chicken is cooked through. Remove the chicken from the slow cooker and shred. Empty the slow cooker and then put the shredded chicken back in. Add the artichoke hearts, garlic, basil, and thyme. Stir well. Place the cream cheese on top of the chicken. Cover and cook on low for 2 hours. Add the cream, water, and flour. Stir well. Cook the pasta according to package directions. You can stir the pasta into the Alfredo sauce or serve it spaghetti-style with the sauce on the top.

# Flavorful Chicken Thighs

| Serves 6 | 6–8 hours on low |
|----------|------------------|

½ cup "less sodium" soy sauce
⅓ cup honey
3 cloves garlic
2 Tbsp. basil
2 Tbsp. balsamic vinegar
1 Tbsp. molasses
2 lb. chicken thighs

These chicken thighs are sure to replace your BBQ chicken recipe. The sauce can be used on chicken breasts as well. Serve the sauce on the side for dipping; it's oh so yummy.

## directions

IN A SMALL bowl, whisk together the soy sauce, honey, garlic, basil, vinegar, and molasses. Place half the chicken along the bottom of the slow cooker and pour half the sauce over the top. Then layer the remaining chicken on top and pour the rest of the sauce over the chicken. Cover and cook on low for 6–8 hours, or until the chicken is cooked through.

# Holiday Chicken

| Serves 6 | 6–8 hours on low |
|----------|------------------|

½ onion, sliced

6 chicken breasts

½ tsp. cinnamon

1 tsp. lemon juice

½ cup orange juice

¼ tsp. cloves

1 (14-oz.) can whole berry cranberry sauce, divided

*I have a good friend who likes to make leftover turkey sandwiches with cranberry sauce. I wasn't a big fan, but his creativity inspired this recipe. I must say, it's pretty great.*

## directions

**ARRANGE THE ONION** in the bottom of the slow cooker. Place the chicken on top of the onion. In a small mixing bowl, stir together the cinnamon, lemon juice, orange juice, and cloves. Reserve ¼ cup of the cranberry sauce and add the rest to the cinnamon mixture. Pour the cinnamon/cranberry sauce over the chicken. Cover and cook on low for 6–8 hours. Garnish with reserved cranberry sauce to serve.

Christina Dymock

# After-School Sliders

| Serves 5 | 4 hours on low |
|----------|----------------|

1 lb. ground turkey
1 tsp. garlic
1 tsp. onion powder
½ tsp. chili powder
¼ tsp. cilantro
10 wheat dinner rolls
assorted burger toppings

I have a three boys, and the older they get, the harder it is to satisfy their hunger. I started making sliders once a week or so for an after-school snack when my oldest was in 8th grade. Not only does it keep them out of the sweets, it gives them protein growing boys can't get enough of.

## directions

PLACE THE TURKEY in the slow cooker. Cover and cook on low for 4 hours. On a plate, mix together the garlic, onion powder, chili powder, and cilantro. Set aside until the meat is done. Once the meat is cooked through, remove it from the slow cooker and roll it in the spices on the plate. Slice the meat into 10 sliders. Place one turkey patty on each roll. Top with your choice of burger toppings and serve.

# One-Pot Baked Potato Bar

| Serves 6 | 2-4 hours on high or 4-6 hours on low |
|---|---|

1 lb. ground turkey

2 Tbsp. olive oil, divided

1 small onion, chopped,

1 (8-oz.) can no-salt-added tomato sauce

1 (15-oz.) can S&W Pinquito Beans with onion and cumin

2 cloves garlic, minced

¼ tsp. pepper

¼ tsp. nutmeg

¼ tsp. paprika

6 medium-sized red potatoes

your choice of toppings

*The fewer dishes I have to wash the better. Since the potatoes and chili cook in the same slow cooker, it drastically reduces kitchen-sink time.*

## directions

**BROWN THE TURKEY** in 1 tablespoon olive oil or use the instructions on page 74 to cook the turkey in the slow cooker and chop it into small pieces. In a medium-sized bowl, combine the turkey, onion, tomato sauce, beans, garlic, pepper, nutmeg, and paprika. Set aside. Use the remaining olive oil to coat the potatoes. Place the potatoes in a large slow cooker. Pour the turkey mixture over the top of the potatoes and cook for 2–4 hours on high or 4–6 hours on low, or until the potatoes are cooked through. Remove the potatoes and cut open the tops. Divide the chili between the potatoes and top with your favorite toppings.

Christina Dymock

# Chicken Tamales

| Serves 8 | 2-3 hours on high |
|----------|-------------------|

*Though they are labor intensive, tamales are always a hit. They are perfect for family dinners or an impressive meal to serve guests. Be sure to soak your husks for at least 20 minutes before rolling the tamales so they don't rip.*

14–16 dried corn husks

3 large chicken breasts, cooked

1 tsp. cumin

1½ tsp. garlic powder

½ tsp. onion powder

¼ tsp. ground mustard

¼ tsp. nutmeg

¼ tsp. ground red pepper (can use more to taste)

A batch of Masa Harina mixed according to package directions

## directions

**SET THE CORN HUSKS** to soak in warm water for 20–30 minutes. Shred the chicken and place it in a large mixing bowl. Add the cumin, garlic powder, onion powder, mustard, nutmeg, and red pepper. Stir well. To assemble the tamales, place a corn husk on a dish towel on the counter. Spoon 2 tablespoons of masa onto the husk and spread it out. Add $\frac{1}{8}$ cup of the chicken mixture. Fold the husk so the masa meets in the middle and press together, sealing the chicken inside the masa. Now, fold up the bottom of the husk, then fold the right side over and then the left, leaving the top open. Shred one of the corn husks into long strips and use a strip to tie off the top of the tamale. Repeat with remaining ingredients. Pour 1½ cups water into the bottom of the slow cooker. Place the tamales inside. Cover and cook on high for 2–3 hours, or until the masa is set and the chicken is heated through.

Christina Dymock

# Pork

# Pork Roast Rub

| Serves 6 | 6–8 hours on low |
|----------|------------------|

2 tsp. oregano

2 tsp. cumin

½ tsp. chili powder

1 tsp. smoked paprika

¼ tsp. salt

¼ tsp. pepper

1 (3- to 4-lb.) pork roast

*I used to think that liquid marinades were the only way to go in the slow cooker. However, once I tried rubs, I got hooked. This one is packed full of flavor—enjoy!*

## directions

**IN A SMALL BOWL,** combine the oregano, cumin, chili powder, paprika, salt, and pepper. Rub the herbs into the meat, coating it evenly. Place the roast in the slow cooker, cover, and cook on low for 6–8 hours, or until the roast is cooked through.

# Moo Shu Pork

| Serves 12 | 4–5 hours on high or 7–8 hours on low |

⅓ cup hoisin sauce

3 cloves garlic, minced

2 Tbsp. dark Asian sesame oil

2 Tbsp. "less sodium" soy sauce

1 Tbsp. cornstarch

a dash of cinnamon

2 carrots, sliced thin

1 head of cabbage, sliced thin

1 lb. boneless pork chops

2 cups broccoli heads

*I don't remember how my kids got hooked on Chinese food, but one day they just fell in love and begged for it. To appease them, I cooked up this slow cooker version of Moo Shu Pork. They loved it, and I hope your family will too.*

## directions

**IN A SMALL BOWL,** combine the hoisin sauce, garlic, sesame oil, soy sauce, cornstarch, and cinnamon. Set aside. Spray the inside of a large slow cooker with nonstick cooking spray. Layer the carrots and cabbage in the slow cooker. Cut the pork chops into thin slices and place them on top of the cabbage. Add the broccoli. Pour the sauce over the top and cover. Cook on high for 4–5 hours or low for 7–8 hours, or until the carrots are soft and the pork is cooked through.

Christina Dymock

# Pepper and Lime Pork Tacos

| Serves 6 | 6–8 hours on low |
|---|---|

1 (3- to 4-lb.) pork roast
½ cup lime juice
½ tsp. black pepper
½ tsp. ground mustard
a pinch of ground red pepper
6–8 whole wheat soft taco shells
2 Roma tomatoes, diced
1 red onion, diced
1 head of lettuce, shredded

*P*epper and lime? Yep. The flavor combination sparkles.

## directions

**PLACE THE ROAST** in the slow cooker. Pour the lime juice over the roast and sprinkle with the black pepper, mustard, and red pepper. Cover and cook on low for 6–8 hours. Once cooked through, remove the meat from the slow cooker and shred. Place a taco shell on a plate and add meat, tomatoes, onion, and lettuce to serve.

# Mexican Pork Chops and Rice

| Serves 6 | 4–6 hours on high or 6–8 hours on low |
|---|---|

1½ cups brown rice

1 (8-oz.) can no-salt-added tomato sauce

2 Roma tomatoes, chopped

½ yellow onion, chopped

1 green pepper, chopped

1 tsp. lime juice

2 tsp. cilantro flakes

¼ tsp. pepper

6 boneless pork chops

1 (15.5-oz.) can low sodium chicken broth

¼ cup water

For those nights you know you won't have time to make a side dish, this recipe makes the rice too.

## directions

**SPRAY THE INSIDE** of a medium-sized slow cooker with nonstick cooking spray. In a medium-sized bowl, stir together the brown rice, tomato sauce, tomatoes, onion, green pepper, lime juice, cilantro, and pepper. Place ⅔ of the rice mixture in the slow cooker. Add the pork chops and cover with the remaining rice mixture. Pour the chicken broth and water down the sides of the slow cooker. Cover and cook on low for 6–8 hours or high for 4–6 hours, or until the rice and pork chops are cooked through.

Christina Dymock

# Pulled Pork Sandwiches

| Serves 8 | 8–10 hours on low |
|----------|-------------------|

3 Tbsp. olive oil

2 cloves garlic, minced

2 tsp. oregano

1½ tsp. cumin

½ tsp. basil

1 (4-lb.) pork shoulder roast

1 navel orange, sliced

1 white onion, sliced

1 jalapeño, seeded and chopped

12–16 pretzel rolls or 8 whole wheat hamburger buns

*This is not your everyday BBQ pork sandwich. It has a kick. I like to serve it on pretzel rolls, like sliders. But it's also good on whole wheat hamburger buns.*

## directions

**COMBINE THE OLIVE OIL**, garlic, oregano, cumin, and basil in a small bowl. Rub the spices over the roast and place the roast in the slow cooker. Add the orange slices, onion, and jalapeño. Cover and cook on low for 8–10 hours or until the meat shreds easily. Remove the roast from the slow cooker and shred. Place it back in the juices to keep warm until serving. Spoon onto pretzel rolls or hamburger buns.

# Red Delicious Pork Chops

| Serves 6 | 6–8 hours on low |
|---|---|

- 4 Tbsp. extra hot prepared horseradish
- 1 tsp. Dijon mustard
- 1 large red delicious apple, peeled and chopped
- 6 sliced thin pork chops
- ¼ cup sour cream
- 1 oz. feta cheese
- 1 cup red grapes, cut in half

*It may seem like a strange combination, but the fruit and feta cheese complement one another. The pork chops can be served without the sauce if you're in a pinch for time. Simply sprinkle the cheese and grapes over the chops and you're ready to go.*

## directions

**IN A SMALL BOWL,** mix together the horseradish, Dijon mustard, and chopped apple. Layer the pork chops and horseradish sauce in the slow cooker. Cover and cook on low for 6–8 hours, or until the pork chops are cooked through. To make the sauce, skim ¼ cup of the juice and apples out of the slow cooker. Add sour cream and feta cheese and mix well. Drizzle over pork chops and sprinkle with cut grapes to serve.

# Tangy Pulled Pork

| Serves 8 | 4-5 hours on high<br>or 8-10 hours on low |
|---|---|

1 (3-lb.) pork roast

½ cup water

¼ cup cider vinegar

2 Tbsp. Worcestershire sauce

1 Tbsp. lime juice

1 tsp. cumin

½ tsp. ground mustard

¼ tsp. nutmeg

½ bunch fresh cilantro

*This is a versatile recipe. It can be served over rice, on its own, or sandwiched between toasted bread.*

## directions

**PLACE THE ROAST** in a large slow cooker. In a small bowl, combine the water, vinegar, Worcestershire sauce, lime juice, cumin, ground mustard, and nutmeg. Pour over the roast. Place the cilantro over the top of the roast. Cover and cook on low 8–10 hours or high 4–5 hours. Once cooked, remove the meat from the slow cooker and shred.

# Pineapple Pork Chops

| Serves 6 | 4-6 hours on high or 6-8 hours on low |
|----------|---------------------------------------|

1 fresh pineapple
6 lean pork chops

Sometimes, the simplicity of a recipe is what makes it stand out. This recipe for Pineapple Pork Chops couldn't be simpler, yet the result is simply delicious.

## directions

**CUT THE PINEAPPLE** into strips and place in a zip-top bag. Add the pork chops. Use a rolling pin to smash the pineapple until it becomes a pulp. Allow the pork chops to marinate for 4 hours or overnight. Dump the whole bag of ingredients into a medium-sized slow cooker. Cover and cook on low for 6–8 hours or high for 4–6 hours.

Christina Dymock

# Red Pepper Pork Chops

| Serves 6 | 6–8 hours on low |
|----------|------------------|

1 tsp. oregano
1 tsp. parsley
½ tsp. dill
2 Tbsp. olive oil
1 tsp. lemon juice
6 sliced thin pork chops
1 red pepper, sliced thin

*Pork chops are sold in different thicknesses. Some are labeled "thick cut" while others are labeled "thin." A thick cut pork chop can be up to a ½ inch thick, while a thin-cut chop will be about ¼ inch thick. Thin-cut pork chops are perfect for smaller children. With the thicker pork chops, they get bites that are too big for their little mouths. These guys are kid-friendly.*

## directions

**IN A SMALL BOWL,** stir together the oregano, parsley, and dill. Pour the olive oil and lemon juice into the bottom of a large slow cooker. Next, layer the pork chops, herbs, and red pepper slices. Cover and cook on low for 6–8 hours, or until the pork chops are cooked through.

# Italian Pork Roast

| Serves 6 | 4-6 hours on high or 6-8 hours on low |
|----------|----------------------------------------|

¼ cup olive oil
1 (3- to 4-lb.) pork roast
1 tsp. pepper
2 Tbsp. dried basil
2 Tbsp. dried oregano
1 tsp. thyme
4 garlic cloves, minced
½ yellow onion, chopped

*F*ill your home with the aroma of Italian cuisine with this pork roast recipe. It goes great with whole wheat garlic bread.

## directions

**POUR THE OLIVE OIL** into a large slow cooker. Place the meat in the slow cooker and roll it to coat it with the oil. Sprinkle the pepper on one side of the roast. Turn the pepper side down and sprinkle the other side with the basil, oregano, thyme, garlic, and onion. Cover and cook on low for 6–8 hours or on high for 4–6 hours, or until the roast is cooked through.

# Teriyaki Pulled Pork

| Serves 8 | 8 ½ – 10 ½ hours on low, total |
|---|---|

1 (4-lb.) pork shoulder roast

½ cup "less sodium" soy sauce

1 (14.5-oz.) can low sodium chicken broth

1 (20-oz.) can pineapple slices, packed in natural juices, drained (reserve juice)

½ tsp. red pepper flakes

2 Tbsp. water

2 Tbsp. cornstarch

8 whole wheat hamburger buns

*Although it is possible to serve these sandwiches without the pineapple slice, the presentation is worth the extra work.*

## directions

**PLACE THE PORK ROAST** in a large slow cooker. In a small bowl, combine the soy sauce, chicken broth, juice from the pineapple slices, and red pepper flakes. Pour mixture over roast, cover, and cook on low for 8–10 hours, or until the meat shreds easily. Remove the meat from the slow cooker and, using two forks, shred. Mix the water and cornstarch together and then pour into the juices in the slow cooker and whisk. Add the shredded meat back to the slow cooker, cover, and cook for 20–30 minutes. Serve on whole wheat hamburger buns with a pineapple slice.

# Beef

# Apple Roast

| Serves 6 | 8–10 hours on low |
|---|---|

1 (4- to 5-lb.) beef chuck roast

1 tsp. Worcestershire sauce

1 tsp. "less sodium" soy sauce

1 Tbsp. apple cider vinegar

1 clove garlic, minced

1 (12-oz.) pkg. baby carrots

2 red delicious apples, sliced thin

*If you want to add a gravy to this roast, the apples bring a great flavor to the sauce. Simply take a quarter cup of cold water in a small saucepan over medium heat and add 1½ tablespoons of cornstarch, stirring until the lumps are gone. Slowly add 2 cups of the juices from the roast to the water and stir until the mixture boils and thickens.*

## directions

PLACE THE ROAST in the slow cooker. In a small bowl, stir together the Worcestershire sauce, soy sauce, apple cider vinegar, and garlic. Pour over the roast. Place the carrots around and on top of the roast. Layer the apple slices over the top. Cover and cook on low for 8–10 hours, or until the roast is tender.

Christina Dymock

# Prime Roast

| Serves 6 | 10–12 hours on low |
|----------|--------------------|

1 (3- to 3½-lb.) chuck roast

1 (12-oz.) pkg. petite carrots

1½ lb. small red potatoes

½ red onion, sliced

½ cup water

⅓ cup prepared horseradish

⅓ cup red wine vinegar

3 cloves garlic, minced

¼ tsp. pepper

Who doesn't love prime rib? This roast is a good second. It's nice to have the carrots and potatoes cook with the meat because they pick up the flavors. You can serve with creamy horseradish sauce if desired.

## directions

PLACE THE ROAST in a slow cooker. Arrange the carrots, potatoes, and onion around the roast. In a small mixing bowl, whisk together the water, horseradish, red wine vinegar, garlic, and pepper. Pour the liquid over the roast and vegetables. Cover and cook on low for 10–12 hours.

# Slow-Cooked Molasses Roast

| Serves 6 | 6–8 hours on low |
|---|---|

1 (3- to 4-lb.) beef or pork roast

½ cup molasses

½ cup pickle juice

1 Tbsp. Dijon mustard

1 Tbsp. onion powder

1 Tbsp. cumin

1 Tbsp. cilantro

1 tsp. red pepper

*The first time I made this roast, I ended up eating a good portion while standing over the slow cooker with a fork. Do not be afraid of the molasses; it creates a gorgeous color and takes the meat to a deep flavor that will have your family hovering around the kitchen in anticipation. I serve it alone or on toasted bread.*

## directions

PLACE THE ROAST in the slow cooker. In a small mixing bowl, combine the molasses, pickle juice, Dijon mustard, onion powder, cumin, cilantro, and red pepper. Pour over the meat and turn the meat several times to coat well. Cover and cook on low for 6–8 hours, or until the roast is cooked through.

Christina Dymock

# Philly Pulled Beef Sandwiches

| Serves 6 | 6-8 hours on low |
|----------|------------------|

1 (2- to 3-lb.) beef roast

½ tsp. pepper

1 (14.5-oz.) can low sodium beef broth

3 peppers, any color, sliced

1 medium onion, sliced

6 wheat hoagie rolls or hamburger buns

6 slices provolone

While you can certainly serve the sandwiches without browning them, broiling the cheese and sandwich tops only takes an added 5–7 minutes and makes a big difference. Including the broiling time, this recipe takes less than 15 minutes to put together once the roast is cooked.

## directions

PLACE THE ROAST in the slow cooker. Sprinkle with pepper. Pour the beef broth into the bottom of the slow cooker. Layer with the sliced peppers and onion. Cover and cook on low for 6–8 hours, or until the meat shreds easily. Divide the meat between the buns. Top with peppers, onion, and cheese. Place the hoagies on a cookie sheet and broil on low for 5–7 minutes, or until cheese melts. If using hamburger buns, place the top of the buns upside down on the cookie sheet so they can brown as the cheese melts over the meat. Serve warm.

# Tender Beef and Veggies

| Serves 6 | 6–8 hours on low |
|----------|------------------|

2 lb. chuck roast

1 (12-oz.) bag mini carrots, cut in half

1 large onion, roughly chopped

2 cloves garlic, minced

1 (15.5-oz.) can low sodium beef broth

1 tsp. thyme

1 tsp. rosemary

½ tsp. pepper

2 bay leaves

 *Quick and hearty, this stew goes well with crusty bread and a snowstorm.*

### directions

**CUT THE CHUCK ROAST** into 1-inch pieces and place in a large slow cooker. Add the carrots, onion, garlic, broth, thyme, rosemary, pepper, and bay leaves. Cover and cook on low for 6–8 hours. Remove the bay leaves before serving.

# Rib Rub

| Serves 6 | 6-8 hours on low |
|----------|------------------|

1 Tbsp. paprika

2 Tbsp. black pepper

1 tsp. ground red pepper

2 tsp. garlic powder

1 tsp. mustard powder

2 tsp. cumin

3–4 lb. beef ribs

½ cup apple cider

3 Tbsp. yellow mustard

¼ cup honey

A different type of ribs, these come out drier. I like the difference. Also, if there's leftovers, they are wonderful on salads.

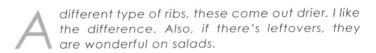

### directions

IN A SMALL BOWL, stir together the paprika, black pepper, red pepper, garlic powder, mustard powder, and cumin. Rub each rib with the dry ingredients and place in the slow cooker. In that same small bowl, combine any leftover seasoning with the apple cider, yellow mustard, and honey. Stir until the honey dissolves. Pour the liquid down the side of the slow cooker. Cover and cook on low for 6–8 hours, or until the ribs are tender and fall apart easily.

# BBQ Ribs with Sauce

| Serves 6 | 6–8 hours on low |
|---|---|

3–3½ lb. beef ribs

½ cup water

3 Tbsp. no-salt-added tomato sauce

2 Tbsp. Worcestershire sauce

3 Tbsp. brown mustard

2 Tbsp. red wine vinegar

2 Tbsp. honey

½ tsp. salt

½ tsp. pepper

So many BBQ recipes call for sugar. This one uses honey instead. We've never missed the refined sugar and thoroughly enjoy the ribs.

## directions

SPRAY A SLOW COOKER with nonstick cooking spray. Place the ribs inside the slow cooker. In a small mixing bowl, combine the water, tomato sauce, Worcestershire sauce, brown mustard, red wine vinegar, honey, salt, and pepper. Pour half the sauce over the ribs, turning each to coat well. Reserve the other half of the sauce in the refrigerator. Cover the ribs and cook on low for 6–8 hours, or until ribs are tender. Remove the ribs from the slow cooker and coat with the reserved sauce to serve.

Christina Dymock

# 1 Pound of Ground Beef

**DO YOU SHY AWAY FROM RECIPES** that ask you to brown the beef or ground turkey because it's such a process? Honestly, the meat has to be thawed, either over-night in the fridge or in the microwave, before it can go into the frying pan. Once on the stove, it can take another 20–30 minutes to brown the meat. Some days, it's just too much.

**INSTEAD OF ALL THAT,** try this technique.

Remove the frozen beef or turkey from the package. Place in a small slow cooker. Cover and cook on high for 4 hours. The meat will remain in the shape it was frozen in, only now, it's cooked through! Simply remove the meat from the slow cooker—leave all those fats behind—and slice or crumble it as needed for your recipe. It's that simple, and it saves what I call "babysitting cooking time." That's the time you have to spend watching food cook. This technique eliminates the need to hover over the meat while it's on the stove top.

*mother-in-law disclaimer*

**MY MOTHER-IN-LAW** had a fit when she heard that I'd placed frozen meat in the slow cooker. ☺ However, my slow cooker gets up to temperature in about 15 min-utes. Once it's hot, it's cooking at around 300 degrees. I wouldn't think twice about throwing frozen meat in the oven at 300 degrees, so I don't worry about it in my slow cooker.

**TO APPEASE** my mother-in-law, whom I love, please be smart when placing frozen foods in your slow cooker. If it heats too slowly, food-borne bacteria can grow and make your family sick. If you're nervous, you can thaw the meat in the microwave and then place it in the slow cooker, on high, for 2 hours.

Christina Dymock

# Soup & Salad

# Jambalaya

| Serves 8 | 4 ½ – 5 ½ hours on low, total |
|---|---|

1 celery rib

½ yellow onion

1 green pepper

3 cloves garlic

1 (14.5-oz.) can no-salt-added diced tomatoes

1 (6-oz.) can no-salt-added tomato sauce

2 cups water

2 cubes reduced sodium chicken bouillon

¼ tsp. pepper

1 tsp. Tabasco sauce (or more to taste)

1 cup long grain rice

2 chicken breasts, cooked and cut into pieces

½ lb. frozen shrimp, thawed

S tep out of your flavor comfort zone and try this spicy dish. If you like it hotter, add an extra dash or two of Tabasco sauce.

## directions

**SLICE THE CELERY** and chop the onion, green pepper, and garlic. Place the veggies in the slow cooker. Add the tomatoes, tomato sauce, water, bouillon cubes, pepper, Tabasco sauce, and rice. Cook on low for 4–5 hours, or until the rice is almost cooked through. Add the chicken and shrimp. Cook for 30-45 minutes, or until the shrimp is thoroughly heated. Serve.

# Shrimp Salad with Rice

| Serves 8 | 3 hours on high |
|----------|-----------------|

2½ cups brown rice

2 tsp. Old Bay Seasoning, divided

1 (14.5-oz.) can low sodium chicken broth

½ cup water

1 (12-oz.) bag of medium-sized shrimp, cooked

6 whole wheat tortilla shells

1 head of lettuce, shredded

sour cream and salsa for garnish

One of my all-time favorite recipes! My mom introduced me to Old Bay Seasoning. You can find it on the baking aisle with the spices.

## directions

**SPRAY A LARGE SLOW COOKER** with nonstick cooking spray. Add the rice and 1½ teaspoons Old Bay Seasoning. Stir together. Add the chicken broth and water. Place the shrimp on top of the rice and sprinkle with the remaining ½ teaspoon of Old Bay Seasoning. Cover and cook on high for 3 hours. Place a wheat tortilla on a plate and layer with rice, shrimp, and shredded lettuce. Garnish with sour cream and salsa if desired.

# Steak Fajita Salad

| Serves 6 | 4 hours 20 minutes on low, total |
|----------|----------------------------------|

2 Tbsp. olive oil

1 yellow pepper, sliced

1 red pepper, sliced

½ yellow onion, sliced

1 lb. eye of round steak

½ tsp. garlic powder

½ tsp. cumin

1 bunch cilantro, divided

¼ cup lime juice

¼ cup water

½ Tbsp. honey

2 cloves garlic

1 (10-oz.) pkg. mixed field greens

12 yellow cherry tomatoes, cut in half

1 avocado

*This recipe can be served as traditional fajitas with the tortilla and all, or it can be served as a salad by following the directions below.*

## directions

**POUR THE OLIVE OIL** over the bottom of the slow cooker. Add the peppers and onion. Trim the fat off the steak and slice it thin. Place the slices in the slow cooker. Sprinkle garlic powder and cumin over the top of the meat. Lay ¼ of the bunch of cilantro over the top of the meat. Cover and cook on low for 4 hours.

**FOR THE SAUCE,** place the lime juice, water, honey, garlic, and ¼ of the cilantro into a blender. Blend well.

**WHEN THE MEAT IS COOKED** through, drain the juice off the meat and veggies. Pour half the sauce over the meat, cover, and cook for 20 minutes. Meanwhile, divide the salad greens and cherry tomatoes between 6 plates. Top with the fajita mixture using extra sauce as a salad dressing. Garnish with avocado and remaining cilantro and serve.

# Island Pork Salad

| Serves 6 | 4-6 hours on low |
|----------|------------------|

1 (2- to 3-lb.) pork roast or 6 thin sliced pork chops

½ tsp. black pepper

1 tsp. cumin

1 tsp. chili powder

1 tsp. cinnamon

**Salad**

4 cups spinach

2 cups chopped iceberg lettuce

1 orange or yellow pepper, sliced

½ cup raisins

1 avocado, cubed

1 (11-oz.) can mandarin oranges, drained

**Dressing**

3 Tbsp. lime juice

1 Tbsp. orange juice

2 Tbsp. Dijon mustard

1 tsp. curry powder

¼ tsp. pepper

¾ cup olive oil

1 Tbsp. honey

*This recipe has everything: protein, greens, and fruit. If you'd like to add cheese, you'll also have dairy.*

## directions

**PLACE THE PORK** in a slow cooker. In a small bowl, mix together the pepper, cumin, chili powder, and cinnamon. Rub into pork. Cover and cook on low for 4–6 hours, or until the meat is cooked through. Remove the meat from the slow cooker and set aside to cool while you prepare the salad. In a large salad bowl, toss the spinach, lettuce, pepper, raisins, avocado pieces, and mandarin oranges. Divide the salad between 6 plates. Cut the pork and divide between the salads.

**TO MAKE THE DRESSING,** place the lime juice, orange juice, Dijon mustard, curry powder, pepper, olive oil, and honey in a container with a tight lid. Cover and shake well. Pour dressing over salads or serve on the side.

# Chicken and Beet Spinach Salad

| Serves 6 | 4 hours on high<br>or 6–8 hours on low |
|----------|----------------------------------------|

2 chicken breasts

3 large beets

1 (10-oz.) bag spinach

½ red pepper, sliced thin

1 cup golden tomatoes, cut in half

2 oz. feta cheese, crumbled

**Dressing**

½ cup balsamic vinegar

4 Tbsp. olive oil

1½ tsp. garlic powder

1 tsp. Italian seasoning

*I won't lie to you, this is one of my favorite salads. Because of the way it's cooked, I can reduce the recipe to one chicken breast and one beet and make it for lunch in my small slow cooker. That way I don't have to share.*

### directions

**WRAP THE CHICKEN** and beets individually in aluminum foil and place in the slow cooker with the chicken on the bottom. Cook on low for 6–8 hours or high for 4 hours, or until the chicken is cooked through. Once the chicken and beets are cooked, divide the spinach, red pepper, tomatoes, and feta cheese between 6 plates. Slice the beets and spread them between the serving plates. Finally, use two forks to shred the chicken and divide it evenly as well. To make the dressing, simply whisk together the balsamic vinegar, olive oil, garlic powder, and Italian seasoning in a small bowl. You can also put it in a salad dressing cruse and shake it. Serve while chicken and beets are still warm.

Christina Dymock

# Spicy Beef Salad with Vinaigrette Dressing

| Serves 6 | 4 hours on low |
|----------|----------------|

1 Tbsp. olive oil

1 tsp. lemon juice

2 lb. flat iron steak

1 tsp. crushed red pepper flakes

5 cloves garlic, minced

**Salad**

1 (10-oz.) bag field greens or spinach

1 yellow pepper, sliced thin

½ cup sliced mushrooms

¼ red onion, sliced thin

**Dressing**

2 Tbsp. honey

⅓ cup red wine vinegar

¼ cup olive oil

½ tsp. basil

¼ tsp. pepper

¼ tsp. salt

*No need to go out to find a good salad, this one beats any restaurant salad hands down!*

## directions

**POUR 1 TABLESPOON** olive oil into the bottom of a large slow cooker. Add the lemon juice. Place the meat in the olive oil mixture and sprinkle with the red pepper flakes and garlic. Cover and cook on low for 4 hours, or until the meat is cooked through.

**TO MAKE THE SALAD,** divide the field greens, yellow pepper, mushrooms, and onion between 6 plates. Slice the beef and divide it as well. Serve with the dressing on the side.

**TO MAKE THE DRESSING,** dissolve the honey in the vinegar. Add the ¼ cup olive oil, basil, pepper, and salt. Stir well.

# Citrus Pork Salad

| Serves 6 | 5–6 hours on low |
|----------|------------------|

1 (2- to 3-lb.) pork roast
½ tsp. pepper
8 cups fresh spinach
1 cup cashews
1 cup sliced carrots
1 red onion, sliced

**Dressing**
⅓ cup olive oil
¼ cup vinegar
2 tsp. "less sodium" soy sauce
1 Tbsp. honey
1 tsp. ginger
¼ tsp. pepper

*With a light citrus touch, this salad will fill you up without making you feel stuffed. Make the dressing when you put the pork in the slow cooker, and then store it in the fridge so the flavors have a chance to blend together.*

## directions

**PLACE THE PORK** in the slow cooker and sprinkle with pepper. Cover and cook on low for 5–6 hours, or until cooked through. Remove the meat from the slow cooker, shred, and set aside.

**TO MAKE THE SALAD,** place the spinach in a large salad bowl, sprinkle with the cashews, carrots, onion, and shredded pork.

**TO MAKE THE DRESSING,** pour the olive oil, vinegar, soy sauce, honey, ginger, and pepper in a container with a tight lid. Cover the container and place it in the fridge until you're ready to serve the salad. Shake the dressing well before serving.

# Veggie Tray Soup

| Serves 10 | 6 ½ hours, total |
|-----------|------------------|

2 Tbsp. butter

4 cups broccoli

3 cups baby carrots, cut in half

1 cup sugar snap peas

1 cup sliced celery

1 sliced green pepper

1 (14.5-oz.) can low sodium chicken broth

2 tsp. garlic powder

1 tsp. onion powder

5 cups whole milk, divided

3 Tbsp. wheat flour

2 Tbsp. cornstarch

Have you ever ordered a veggie tray for a party and had tons left over? This recipe is forgiving enough that you can use almost any veggies. If your veggie tray has baby tomatoes, leave those out; but, any veggie, from broccoli to green onions, is fair game.

## directions

**PLACE THE BUTTER,** broccoli, carrots, peas, celery, green pepper, chicken broth, garlic powder, and onion powder in a large slow cooker. Cover and cook on low for 6 hours. After the veggies have cooked, pour 1 cup milk, wheat flour, and cornstarch into a large saucepan. Whisk together until smooth. Place the saucepan over medium heat and stir continually. Once the sauce thickens, slowly add the remaining milk. This will create a thick cream sauce for the soup. Add the sauce to the slow cooker and stir well. Cover, turn the slow cooker up to high, and cook for another 30 minutes.

# Chicken Tortilla Soup

| Serves 6 | 6–8 hours on low |
|---|---|

3 chicken breasts

1 (12-oz.) pkg. frozen corn

1 (14.5-oz.) can no-salt-added pinto beans, rinsed and drained

1 yellow onion, diced

1 jalapeño, diced

3 cloves garlic, minced

3 cups water

3 cubes reduced sodium chicken bouillon

1 Tbsp. cumin

¼ tsp. chili powder

1 tsp. cilantro

¼ tsp. nutmeg

Tortilla soup is a mainstay in most households. Everyone has their own twist on the recipe and this is mine. If you like your tortilla soup a little on the spicy side, try adding more chili powder, but do it in small increments so you don't end up with "dragon soup."

### directions

**PLACE THE CHICKEN BREASTS** in the slow cooker. Add all the remaining ingredients. Cover and cook on low for 6–8 hours, or until the chicken is cooked through. Use two forks to shred the chicken before serving.

# Carrot Soup

| Serves 8 | 6½–8½ hours, total |
|----------|--------------------|

2 Tbsp. olive oil

3 lb. carrots, sliced

2 Tbsp. chopped fresh ginger

1 green onion, chopped

5 cups water

6 cubes reduced sodium chicken bouillon

½ tsp. salt

1 tsp. pepper

2 Tbsp. honey

1 Tbsp. butter

½ cup cream

*D*on't knock it until you try it. Seriously. I was shocked that my younger kids gobbled this up. But then, as babies, they loved pureed carrots so it kind of made sense. Not only did my kids love it, I loved it, and I hope you will too.

## directions

**IN A LARGE SLOW COOKER,** combine the olive oil, carrots, ginger, onion, water, bouillon cubes, salt, pepper, and honey. Cover and cook on low for 6–8 hours. Once cooked through, place the ingredients in a blender and puree. Place the carrot mixture back in the slow cooker. Add the butter and cream, stirring constantly. Cover and cook on high for 15–30 minutes.

# Spinach and Rice Soup

| Serves 8 | 6 hours 20 minutes on low |
|---|---|

- 1 (13-oz.) box vegetable broth
- 1 (8-oz.) can tomato paste
- 1 (15-oz.) can no-salt-added great white northern beans, drained and rinsed
- 1 Tbsp. onion powder
- 1 tsp. basil
- ¼ tsp. salt
- ¼ tsp. black pepper
- 6 garlic cloves
- ½ cup brown rice
- 6 cups chopped fresh spinach
- parmesan cheese for garnish

 A thick soup with spinach, rice, and beans, this dish can hold its own as the main course.

### directions

**POUR THE VEGETABLE BROTH,** tomato paste, and beans into the slow cooker. Add the onion powder, basil, salt, pepper, garlic cloves, and rice. Cover and cook on low for 6 hours. Add the spinach and cook for an additional 20 minutes. Garnish with parmesan cheese to serve.

# Pumpkin Soup

| Serves 10 | 8-10 hours on low |
|---|---|

1 small pumpkin

2 (14.5-oz.) cans low sodium chicken broth

1 onion, chopped

2 cloves garlic

½ tsp. pepper

¼ cup pecans for garnish

Why are pumpkins magical for kids? Is it because they can turn into jack-o'-lanterns, breads, cookies, and pancakes? With this recipe, they also turn into a remarkable soup.

## directions

**WASH AND DRY PUMPKIN.** Remove the seeds and stem and chop into 2–3 inch cubes. Place in a large slow cooker. Add the chicken broth, onion, garlic, and pepper. Cover and cook on low for 8–10 hours, or until the pumpkin is soft. Once the pumpkin is cooked through, put half the mixture in the blender and puree. Repeat with the second half of the mixture. Garnish with pecans to serve.

# Butternut Squash Soup

| Serves 10 | 6-8 hours on low, total |
|-----------|-------------------------|

2 Tbsp. olive oil

1 cup chopped yellow onion

1 large butternut squash, cut into cubes

4 granny smith apples, peeled and chopped

2 Tbsp. mild curry powder

2 cloves garlic, minced

1 tsp. salt

½ tsp. pepper

2 cups water

2 cups apple juice

¼ cup cream

*S*ince the Butternut Squash Chili turned out so good, I decided to try butternut squash on its own. The result was a wonderful, creamy soup that's perfect for the day of that first fall frost.

### directions

**PLACE THE OLIVE OIL,** onion, butternut squash, and apples in the slow cooker. Cover and cook on low for 4–6 hours. Once cooked through, puree the mixture and return it to the slow cooker. Stir in the curry powder, garlic, salt, pepper, water, apple juice, and cream. Stir well, cover, and cook on low for 2 hours.

Christina Dymock

# Butternut Squash Chili

| Serves 8 | 6–8 hours on low |
|----------|------------------|

1 lb. lean ground turkey

1 medium-sized butternut squash, peeled, seeded, and cubed

1 large carrot, sliced

2 celery ribs, sliced

½ red onion, chopped

1 yellow onion, chopped

4 cloves garlic, chopped

1 (15.5-oz.) can no-salt-added pinto beans, rinsed and drained

1 (14.5-oz.) can diced tomatoes

1 (6-oz.) can no-salt-added tomato sauce

2 tsp. beef granules

1½ cups water

1 tsp. oregano

½ tsp. red pepper

*S*urprisingly delicious, the squash makes a wonderful addition to this easy chili.

## directions

**PLACE THE MEAT** in the bottom of the slow cooker. Add all the remaining ingredients. Cover and cook on low for 6–8 hours. Stir well before serving. If needed, use two forks to pull apart the meat and make smaller pieces.

# Hearty Soup

| Serves 6 | 8 hours on low |
|---|---|

- 1 (14-oz.) organic smoked sausage
- 1 sweet potato
- 2 large red potatoes
- 3 green onions
- 2 celery ribs
- 1 bunch of broccoli
- 1 (14.5-oz.) can beef stock

Sausage is full of flavor. Instead of trying to compete with it, use it to its full advantage in this savory soup.

## directions

**SLICE THE SAUSAGE** on the diagonal and place it in the slow cooker. Chop the sweet potato, red potatoes, onion, celery, and broccoli. Add to the slow cooker. Pour in the beef stock, cover, and cook on low for 8 hours.

Christina Dymock

# Chicken and Kale Soup

| Serves 6 | 6 ½ – 8 ½ hours on low, total |
|---|---|

3 chicken breasts

1 yellow onion, chopped

2 celery ribs, chopped

1 tsp. thyme

½ tsp. fresh rosemary

3 Tbsp. fresh parsley

4 (14.5-oz.) can low sodium chicken broth

1 (15.5-oz.) no salt added cannellini beans, drained

4 cups kale (sliced thin with the ribs removed)

Kale can be bitter when eaten raw, but when cooked, it loses that bite. It's super good for you and looks beautiful in this soup.

## directions

**PLACE THE CHICKEN,** onion, celery, thyme, rosemary, and parsley into a large slow cooker. Add the chicken broth, cover, and cook on low for 6-8 hours. Use a large wooden spoon to break the chicken up into smaller pieces, or remove the chicken from the slow cooker and use two forks to shred before returning it to the soup. Add the beans and kale to the soup and cook for an additional 20–30 minutes.

# Memphis Chili

| Serves 8 | 4–6 hours on low |
|----------|------------------|

1 lb. lean ground beef

6 slices turkey bacon, chopped

1 (8-oz.) can tomato paste

1 cup water

1 tsp. chili powder (or more to taste)

½ tsp. turmeric

1 tsp. smoked paprika

1 tsp. celery seed

2 Tbsp. molasses

1 (15.5-oz.) can red beans, drained and rinsed

A hearty chili is always welcome on a fall day, but why not surprise your family after a summer rain?

## directions

**BROWN THE BEEF** or use the directions on page 74 to cook the meat. Place the browned beef, turkey bacon, tomato paste, water, chili powder, turmeric, smoked paprika, celery seed, molasses, and beans in a large slow cooker. Stir until just combined. Cover and cook on low for 4–6 hours.

Christina Dymock

# Sides

# Golden Potato Salad

| Serves 8 | 6–8 hours on low |
|----------|------------------|

1½ lb. golden potatoes
2 Tbsp. olive oil
¼ cup light mayonnaise
3 Tbsp. yellow mustard
3 Tbsp. pickle juice
1 tsp. pepper
1 tsp. Worcestershire sauce

*P*otato salad doesn't have the best of reputations. This version is my way of indulging in good food without feeling guilty about it.

## directions

WASH AND DRY THE POTATOES. Brush each potato with olive oil. I like to pour a little oil in my palms and then roll the potatoes between them, replenishing the oil as needed. Place the potatoes in the slow cooker, cover, and cook on low for 6–8 hours or until the potatoes are cooked through but not soggy. In a large bowl, mix together the mayonnaise, mustard, pickle juice, pepper, and Worcestershire sauce. Once the potatoes are cooked, cut them into cubes and place in the bowl with the sauce. Stir to coat and serve warm or refrigerate for 4 hours and serve cold.

# Beets with Creamy Balsamic Sauce

| Serves 8 | 6 hours on low |
|----------|----------------|

4 large beets
¼ cup balsamic vinegar
¼ cup sour cream

My kids like to eat the beets plain, but I love them with the sauce. If you want to kick up the flavor one more notch, try sprinkling them with crumbled feta cheese.

## directions

WASH AND PREPARE THE BEETS by cutting off their stems and roots. Wrap each beet individually in aluminum foil. I like to wrap mine like peppermint candies with the ends twisted instead of folded. They look great on the plate before they are opened. Place the wrapped beets in a large slow cooker, cover, and cook on low for 6 hours. To make the sauce, whisk together the vinegar and sour cream. Drizzle over the beets or simply place on the table and let everyone drizzle their own.

Christina Dymock

# Not-Just-Rice Pilaf

| Serves 8 | 8 hours on low |
|----------|----------------|

$\frac{2}{3}$ cup white wheat

$\frac{1}{2}$ cup barley

$\frac{3}{4}$ cup wild rice

$\frac{1}{2}$ cup chopped onion

2 (14.5-oz.) cans low sodium chicken broth

1 Tbsp. butter, cut into small cubes

1 tsp. freshly ground garlic pepper seasoning

With this recipe, I can sneak some barley and whole wheat into my kids' day and they don't even notice.

## directions

IN A LARGE SLOW COOKER, stir together the wheat, barley, wild rice, and onion. Add the chicken broth, butter, and garlic pepper seasoning. Cover and cook on low for 8 hours.

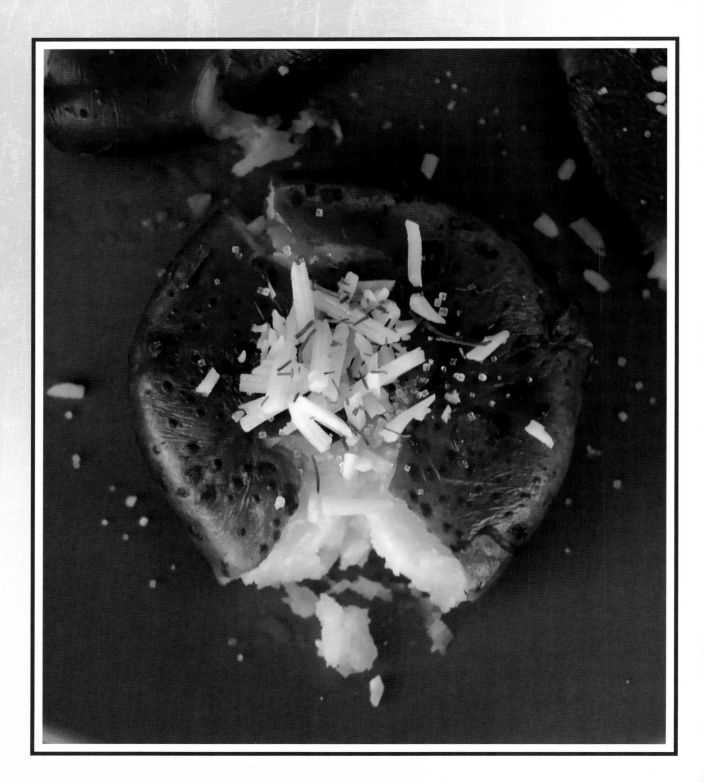

# Smashed Potatoes

| Serves 6 | 6-8 hours on low |
|---|---|

6 red potatoes

1 Tbsp. olive oil

¼ tsp. pepper

¼ tsp. Season All seasoning

½ cup shredded cheddar cheese, optional

My son kept asking for "smashed potatoes." In my ignorance, I thought that was his cute way of saying "mashed potatoes." One day I made baked potatoes and watched as he smashed it with his fork and then ate it happily. He really did want smashed potatoes. Here they are, hope your kids love them too. Feel free to let the kids do the smashing.

## directions

**WASH AND DRY THE POTATOES.** Cover each with a coating of olive oil. I pour a little of the olive oil into the palm of my hands and then roll the potato around in my palms. Place the potatoes in a slow cooker, cover, and cook on low for 6–8 hours. Once the potatoes are done, transfer them to a cookie sheet. Use the bottom of a heavy plate or drinking glass to smash the potatoes flat. Sprinkle each potato with pepper, Season All, and cheddar cheese (if desired) before serving.

# Cajun Rice with Shrimp

| Serves 8 | 5–6 ½ hours on low, total |
|----------|---------------------------|

2 large tomatoes, diced

½ yellow onion, chopped

1 yellow pepper, chopped

2 cloves garlic, chopped

2 cubes reduced sodium chicken bouillon, crushed

1 cup whole grain brown rice

2 cups water

¾ tsp. Creole seasoning

1 lb. cooked, shelled, and deveined shrimp

Having a hearty side dish is important when serving a family. Picky eaters may not go for the main dish, but they load up on the other foods on the table. With the shrimp in this recipe, you'll know they are getting some protein in their picky diets.

### directions

IN A LARGE SLOW COOKER, mix together the tomatoes, onion, pepper, garlic, crushed bouillon cubes, brown rice, water, and Creole seasoning. Cook on low for 5–6 hours. Add shrimp and cook for 15–20 minutes more.

Christina Dymock

# Spaghetti Squash

| Serves 8 | 6–8 hours on low |
|---|---|

1 (2- to 3-lb.) spaghetti squash
2 cups water
2–4 Tbsp. butter
salt and pepper

Spaghetti squash is pretty versatile. It can be covered with tomato sauce and served as a main dish, or lightly sprinkled with seasoning and served as a side dish as it is here.

## directions

WASH THE SPAGHETTI SQUASH. Use a knife or fork to puncture the squash several times and place it in a slow cooker. Add water. Cover and cook on low for 6–8 hours. Once cooked, take the squash out of the slow cooker and allow to cool for 10–15 minutes or until you can handle it without burning yourself. Slice the squash in half and remove the seeds. Scrape out the spaghetti strands and divide them between the plates. Top with a small pat of butter and add salt and pepper to taste.

Christina Dymock

# Fresh Green Beans

| Serves 6 | 8-10 hours on low |
|----------|-------------------|

1 lb. green beans
1 Tbsp. lemon juice
3 cups water
salt and pepper

*I have awesome neighbors who garden like champs. Thankfully, they are willing to share their bounty. This simple green beans recipe was inspired by a grocery bag full of freshly picked green beans. If you don't have a garden, or awesome neighbors, store-bought beans will work just fine.*

## directions

RINSE THE BEANS and snip the ends. Place in a slow cooker. Add the lemon juice and water. Cover and cook on low for 8–10 hours. Salt and pepper to taste and serve.

----------------------------- SIDES -----------------------------

# Salmon Rolls

| Serves 6 | 4-6 hours on low |
|----------|------------------|

5 cups water

1 head green cabbage

1 (14.75-oz.) can salmon, drained with skin and bones removed

2 eggs

1 ⅓ cup Italian-style bread crumbs

¼ tsp. lemon pepper

½ cup low sodium chicken broth

*W*hile this is a wonderful side dish, I've also served Salmon Rolls as a main dish. Simply mix up a batch of ham fried rice to serve alongside and you have a filling and healthy meal.

## directions

THE WATER TO BOIL in a large stockpot. Cut off the cabbage stem so that it's even with the cabbage head. Place the cabbage in the boiling water for 10–15 minutes or until the leaves are soft and easy to peel away. While the cabbage is cooking, combine the salmon, eggs, bread crumbs, and lemon pepper in a medium-sized mixing bowl. Set aside. Pour the chicken broth into the bottom of a slow cooker. When the cabbage is done, remove it from the water and peel off a leaf. Scoop 2 tablespoons of the salmon mixture onto a leaf and then roll it in, tucking in the sides. Place the roll in the slow cooker and repeat with remaining cabbage leaves and salmon mixture. Cover and cook on low for 4–6 hours, or until rolls are cooked through.

# Steak Restaurant Mushrooms

| Serves 6 | 4-5 hours on low |
|----------|------------------|

1 head garlic
16 oz. whole mushrooms
1 Tbsp. butter, melted
2 Tbsp. Worcestershire sauce
1 Tbsp. balsamic vinegar

You know those mushrooms you can get on top of a thick, juicy steak? These are those mushrooms. As a bonus, the recipe also makes a delicious roasted garlic clove.

## directions

SPRAY A SLOW COOKER with nonstick cooking spray. Cut the top off the garlic and remove the papery outer layers. Place in the center of the slow cooker. Wash the mushrooms and slice. Place around the garlic in the slow cooker. Pour the melted butter, Worcestershire sauce, and balsamic vinegar over the top. Cover and cook on low for 4–5 hours.

Christina Dymock

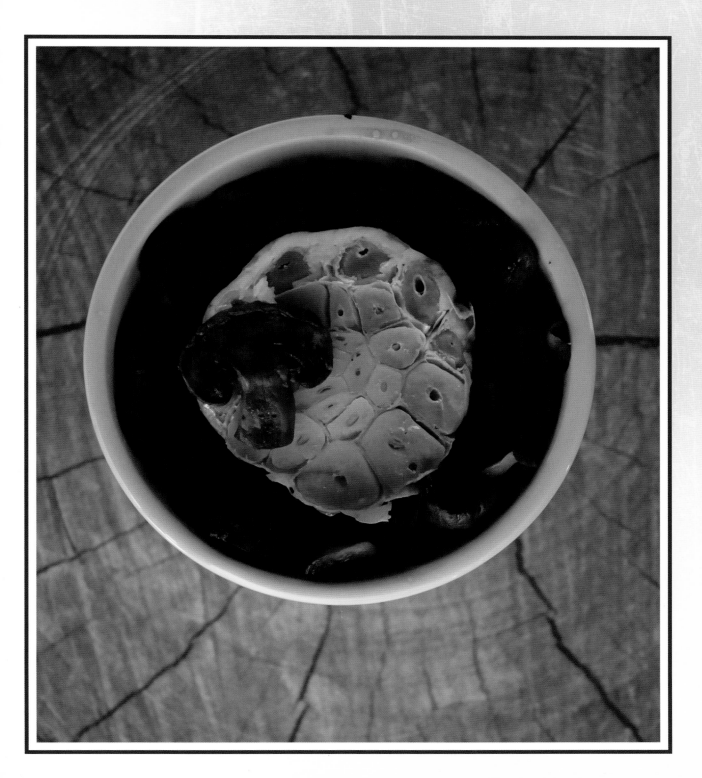

# Beans and Rice

| Serves 12 | 5-7 hours on high, total |
|---|---|

- 1 (16-oz.) bag dry pinto beans
- 1 (8-oz.) can no-salt-added tomato sauce
- 2 Tbsp. molasses
- 1 tsp. pepper
- 4 cloves garlic, minced
- ½ tsp. chili powder
- 1 tsp. cumin
- 1 tsp. oregano
- 1 Tbsp. cocoa
- 1 bay leaf
- 1 cup brown rice

*Not only does this dish work well as a side dish, it can double as a vegetarian taco dinner. Simply serve with wheat tortillas, shredded lettuce, and other taco toppings. The flavor is great and it's filling.*

## directions

RINSE THE BEANS and place in a large slow cooker. Add water to cover the beans by 2 inches. Add the tomato sauce, molasses, pepper, garlic, chili powder, cumin, oregano, cocoa, and bay leaf. Cover and cook for 3–4 hours on high. Add the rice and cook for 2–3 more hours, or until the rice and beans are tender. Remove the bay leaf to serve.

# Slow Cooker Artisan Bread

| Serves 8 | 2-3 hours on low |
|----------|------------------|

1 ½ cups flour
1 ½ cups wheat flour
1 tsp. salt
1 tsp. active dry yeast
1 ½ cups water

*This recipe is great plain, but I often like to add ¼ cup sunflower seeds to the batter before adding the water so the seeds are distributed well.*

## directions

IN A LARGE BOWL, stir together the flour, wheat flour, salt, and yeast. Make a well in the flour mixture and pour in the water. Use a fork to stir the dough together until it becomes sticky. Cover the bowl with plastic wrap and allow to rise 8 hours or overnight. Scrape the dough onto a lightly floured surface. Pull each side up and over, pushing it down in the center to gently knead the dough and shape it into a ball. Line a slow cooker with parchment paper. Place the dough inside the slow cooker. Cover and cook on low for 2–3 hours, or until the top of the bread is firm.

# Wheat Bread

| Serves 8 | 2½ hours on low |
| --- | --- |

2½ tsp. active dry yeast
1 cup warm water
2 cups wheat flour
1 cup white flour
¼ tsp. salt
2 Tbsp. olive oil
2 Tbsp. honey

*There is nothing quite like homemade bread. It's like love in a loaf. Serve this with the Carrot Soup on page 95 or the Chicken and Asparagus Dinner on page 8.*

## directions

IN A SMALL BOWL, dissolve the yeast in the warm water. In a medium-sized mixing bowl, combine the flours and salt. Use a fork to stir in the olive oil and honey. Once bubbles form on top of the yeast-water, pour the liquid into the bowl and used a fork to stir it all together. The dough will be sticky. Turn the dough out onto a lightly floured surface. Dust your hands with flour and knead the dough for 5–7 minutes or until the dough is smooth and elastic. Place back in the bowl, cover with a damp cloth, and allow to rise until double in size. Punch down the dough. Line a slow cooker with parchment paper. Place the dough in the slow cooker, cover, and cook on low for 2½ hours, or until the edges are brown and the top is firm.

Christina Dymock

# Mashed Cauliflower

| Serves 8 | 6-8 hours on low |
|----------|------------------|

- 1 head cauliflower, cut into large florets
- 1 cup low sodium chicken broth
- 1 Tbsp. butter
- ¼ cup milk
- ½ cup parmesan cheese
- ½ tsp. pepper

One of the great things about this dish is the way it smells when it's cooking. It's one of those aromas that leads people to the kitchen to find out what's cooking.

## directions

PLACE THE CAULIFLOWER and chicken broth in a slow cooker. Cover and cook on low for 6–8 hours. When the cauliflower is tender, drain the chicken broth and place the cauliflower in a large mixing bowl. Add the butter, milk, parmesan cheese, and pepper. Use a potato masher to combine the ingredients and smash the cauliflower. When the lumps are gone, serve.

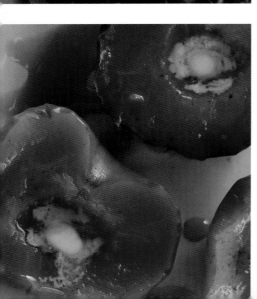

# Sweet Endings

# Apple Dump Cake

| Serves 8 | 2-2½ hours on high |
|----------|--------------------|

2 gala apples, cored, peeled, and sliced

½ cup walnuts (optional)

½ cup golden raisins

1 tsp. cinnamon

1 cup flour

¼ cup sugar substitute or the equivalent of ¼ cup sugar

1 tsp. baking powder

¼ tsp. salt

½ cup milk

3 Tbsp. butter, melted and divided

1 tsp. vanilla

1 cup apple juice

⅓ cup organic brown sugar

*This cake comes out sweet. The batter is thick, so I use a spoon and drop it over the apples like dumplings. It is good plain, with all-natural whipped cream, or with sugar-free ice cream.*

## directions

SPRAY A LARGE SLOW COOKER with nonstick cooking spray. Spread the apples, walnuts (optional), and golden raisins along the bottom of the slow cooker. Sprinkle the cinnamon over the apples. In a small bowl, mix together the flour, sugar substitute, baking powder, salt, milk, 2 tablespoons melted butter, and vanilla. Drop by spoonful over the apple mixture. Combine the apple juice, brown sugar, and 1 tablespoon of melted butter in a small mixing bowl until the brown sugar dissolves. Pour over the top of the mixture in the slow cooker. Cover and cook on high for 2–2½ hours, or until a knife inserted in the cake comes out clean. Serve warm.

# Sugar-Free Chocolate Bread Pudding

| Serves 6 | 2 ½ hours on high |
|----------|-------------------|

3 cups milk

½ cup sugar-free fudge topping

⅓ cup cocoa powder

¼ cup sugar substitute or the equivalent of ¼ cup sugar

3 eggs

5 cups bread cubes

½ cup walnuts (optional)

sugar-free chocolate sauce or fudge topping

*B*ecause this recipe has a high chocolate-to-sweet ratio, my kids prefer it drizzled with extra sugar-free chocolate sauce. I've written that into the recipe. You could also use all-natural whipped cream and chocolate shavings if you desire.

## directions

SPRAY THE INSIDE of a large slow cooker with nonstick cooking spray. Set aside. In a medium-sized sauce pan, heat the milk until small bubbles appear around the edges but do not bring to a boil. Remove from heat and add the fudge topping, cocoa powder, and sugar substitute. Stir until the fudge topping incorporates into the milk. Beat in the eggs and set aside. Place the bread cubes in a large mixing bowl. Pour the chocolate mixture over the bread cubes and stir to coat. Transfer the mixture to the prepared slow cooker. Cover and cook on high for 2½ hours. Drizzle with additional chocolate sauce and sprinkle with walnuts if desired.

# Baked Apples

| Serves 8 | 2-2½ hours on high |
|---|---|

4 large red delicious apples

a pinch of cinnamon

sugar-free caramel topping, whipped cream, chopped walnuts, or your choice of toppings

*A*pples do well in a slow cooker. The gradual cook time hones the natural sugars in the fruit to the perfect flavor. You can drizzle them with sugar-free caramel sauce or serve them with a dollop of whipped cream.

## directions

SLICE THE APPLES in half and remove the seeds. Place in a slow cooker, cut side up. Cover and cook on low for 2–3 hours, or until cooked through. Sprinkle with cinnamon and add desired toppings. Serve immediately.

Christina Dymock

# Cookie Bars

| Serves 6 | 2-2½ hours |
|---|---|

½ cup butter, melted

¾ cup sugar substitute, or the equivalent of ¾ cup sugar

2 eggs

1 tsp. vanilla

¼ tsp. salt

2 cups flour

½ cup pecans, roughly chopped

1 cup chocolate pieces

*Have you ever put off making cookies because you didn't want to stand around the kitchen, waiting to switch out cookie sheets? With these delicious cookie bars, you don't have to babysit. Just pop them in the slow cooker and get back to your life. In a couple hours, you'll have delicious cookies.*

## directions

LINE A SLOW COOKER with aluminum foil. Spray the foil with nonstick cooking spray and set aside. In a large mixing bowl, combine the butter, sugar equivalent, and eggs. Add the vanilla, salt, and flour. Use a hand mixer to beat together until just combined. Add the nuts and chocolate pieces. Transfer the dough to the prepared slow cooker and spread evenly. Place two paper towels over the top of the slow cooker and secure in place with the lid. Cook for 2–2½ hours, or until the cookie is set in the middle. Once done, immediately use the aluminum foil to lift the cookie from the slow cooker. Place cookie on a wire rack to cool for 30–60 minutes before serving.

# Chocolate Cake

| Serves 8 | 4–5 hours on low |
|---|---|

- 2½ cups flour
- ⅓ cup cocoa powder
- ⅓ cup dark cocoa powder
- 1 tsp. baking soda
- ½ tsp. salt
- ¾ cup sugar substitute, or the equivalent of ¾ cup sugar
- ½ cup coconut oil
- 2 eggs
- 1 tsp. vanilla
- 1 (6-oz.) container Greek yogurt
- ⅓ cup unsweetened shredded coconut
- ½ cup sugar-free caramel ice cream topping

*Yep—sugar-free chocolate cake. I had a friend on a sugar-free diet and wanted to take her a thank-you gift. This cake was perfect. She couldn't believe it was sugar-free, but that didn't stop her from eating it.*

### directions

IN A LARGE BOWL, sift together the flour, cocoa powders, baking soda, salt, and sugar substitute. Make a well in the flour mixture and add the coconut oil, eggs, vanilla, and Greek yogurt. Beat well. Batter will be sticky. Pour into a greased and floured slow cooker and even off the top. Sprinkle with the coconut. Cover and cook on low for 4–5 hours, or until a toothpick inserted in the center comes out clean. Drizzle with sugar-free caramel ice cream topping to serve.

# Blueberry Pudding Cake

| Serves 6 | 2½–3 hours on high |
|----------|--------------------|

1 cup fresh blueberries

3 eggs at room temperature

½ cup sugar substitute, or the equivalent of ½ cup of sugar

½ cup flour

1 tsp. vanilla

¼ tsp. salt

1 cup milk

3 Tbsp. lemon juice

3 Tbsp. butter at room temperature

I've used both lemon juice and lime juice in this recipe and loved both flavors. If you'd like to try the lime, simply omit the lemon juice and use 3 tablespoons of lime juice instead. To get your eggs to room temperature, you can place them in a bowl and run lukewarm water over them until they lose their chill.

## directions

SPRAY A MEDIUM-SIZED SLOW COOKER with nonstick cooking spray. Spread the blueberries over the bottom of the slow cooker. Set aside. Separate eggs, yolks in one bowl and whites in the other. Add the sugar substitute, flour, vanilla, salt, milk, lemon juice, and butter to the bowl with the egg yolks. Mix well. Beat the egg whites until soft peaks form. Fold the whites into the cake batter. Transfer the mixture to the slow cooker, covering the blueberries. Cover and cook on high for 2½–3 hours.

# Carrot Cake with Cream Cheese Glaze

| Serves 8 | 3-4 hours on high |
|---|---|

2 cups grated carrots (3–4 large carrots)

1 (20-oz.) can pineapple slices packed in 100% juice, chopped

½ cup chopped pecans or walnuts

¾ cup unsweetened coconut

3 large eggs

½ cup oil

½ cup applesauce

2 cups flour

2 tsp. cinnamon

¼ tsp. cloves

2 tsp. baking soda

¼ tsp. salt

1 tsp. baking powder

Glaze

2 Tbsp. butter, melted

2 oz. cream cheese at room temperature

1 cup sugar substitute, or the equivalent of 1 cup sugar

1 tsp. vanilla

4 Tbsp. milk

O h yeah, it's sugar-free and packed full of flavor.

## directions

LINE A LARGE SLOW COOKER with aluminum foil. Spray with nonstick cooking spray and set aside. In a large mixing bowl, combine the carrots, pineapple, nuts, and coconut. Add the eggs, oil, and applesauce and stir. Add the flour, cinnamon, cloves, baking soda, salt, and baking powder. Stir until well combined. Pour into the prepared slow cooker, cover, and bake on high for 3–4 hours, or until a toothpick inserted in the center comes out clean.

FOR GLAZE: beat the butter and cream cheese until creamy. Add the sweetener, vanilla, and milk. Beat until smooth. Drizzle over carrot cake to serve.

Christina Dymock

# Blueberry Crisp Ice Cream Topper

| Serves 6 | 3-5 hours on low |
|----------|------------------|

12 oz. frozen blueberries

1½ cup quick oats

¼ cup chopped pecans

½ cup whole wheat flour

½ tsp. salt

⅓ cup raw honey

4 Tbsp. butter at room temperature

Serve this deep-flavored ice cream topper with sugar-free vanilla ice cream for the perfect ending to any meal.

## directions

SPRAY A LARGE SLOW COOKER with nonstick cooking spray. Place the blueberries in the bottom of the slow cooker. Set aside. In a mixing bowl, combine the oats, pecans, whole wheat flour, salt, honey, and butter with a hand mixer until the mixture is crumbly, 2–3 minutes. Sprinkle the oat mixture over the blueberries. Spread evenly. Cover and cook on low for 3–5 hours. Serve over ice cream.

# Simple Banana Custard

| Serves 8 | 3–4 hours on high |
|----------|-------------------|

3 eggs

2 yellow bananas

1 (13.5-oz.) can unsweetened coconut milk

1 tsp. vanilla

a pinch of cinnamon

In order to get all the ramekins in the slow cooker, I have to layer them. If you can't get them all in, feel free to cook them in two batches, or you can use two slow cookers. It's a good idea to do a dry run to see how yours will fit before you start.

## directions

IN A MEDIUM BOWL, beat the eggs, bananas, coconut milk, and vanilla together. Pour the batter into 8 ramekins. Place ramekins in the slow cooker. Pour water down the side of the slow cooker until the water reaches halfway up the bottom ramekins. Cover and cook on high for 3–4 hours, or until the custard is set in the center. Sprinkle with cinnamon and serve.

# Citrus Ice Cream Topper

| Serves 8 | 2½ – 3½ hours on high |
| --- | --- |

- 2 large oranges, peeled and sliced
- 1 pear, peeled and sliced
- 1 lemon, peeled and sliced
- 3 Tbsp. sugar substitute or the equivalent of 3 Tbsp. of sugar
- ⅓ cup orange juice
- 1 Tbsp. cornstarch
- 1 tsp. vanilla

*The mellow orange flavor of this ice cream topper works well with sugar-free vanilla ice cream. However, there is something to be said about the combination of chocolate and orange. Feel free to offer your family or guests a choice. They might just surprise you.*

## directions

SPRAY THE INSIDE of a slow cooker with non-stick cooking spray. Add the oranges, pear, and lemon to the slow cooker. Sprinkle with the sugar substitute. In a small bowl, mix the orange juice and cornstarch together. Pour over the fruit. Cover and cook on high for 2–3 hours. It should be thick. If it hasn't thickened, take the lid off and let cook for another 20–30 minutes. Add the vanilla and stir well. Serve over ice cream.

# Cooking Measurement Equivalents

| Cups | Tablespoons | Fluid Ounces |
|---|---|---|
| ⅛ cup | 2 Tbsp. | 1 fl. oz. |
| ¼ cup | 4 Tbsp. | 2 fl. oz. |
| ⅓ cup | 5 Tbsp. + 1 tsp. | |
| ½ cup | 8 Tbsp. | 4 fl. oz. |
| ⅔ cup | 10 Tbsp. + 2 tsp. | |
| ¾ cup | 12 Tbsp. | 6 fl. oz. |
| 1 cup | 16 Tbsp. | 8 fl. oz. |

| Cups | Fluid Ounces | Pints/Quarts/Gallons |
|---|---|---|
| 1 cup | 8 fl. oz. | ½ pint |
| 2 cups | 16 fl. oz. | 1 pint = ½ quart |
| 3 cups | 24 fl. oz. | 1½ pints |
| 4 cups | 32 fl. oz. | 2 pints = 1 quart |
| 8 cups | 64 fl. oz. | 2 quarts = ½ gallon |
| 16 cups | 128 fl. oz. | 4 quarts = 1 gallon |

## Other Helpful Equivalents

| | |
|---|---|
| 1 Tbsp | 3 tsp. |
| 8 oz. | ½ lb. |
| 16 oz. | 1 lb. |

# Index

# the Healthy Family
## slow cooker
### COOKBOOK

_____

_____

_____

_____

_____

_____

_____

_____

_____

_____

# About the Author

Christina Dymock is the author of *The Hungry Family Slow Cooker Cookbook*, *The Bacon Lover's Cookbook*, *One Dirty Bowl: Fast Baking, Faster Cleanup*, and several other cookbooks. She has also written for *Deseret News* and been interviewed for *Parents' Magazine* and other national publications. Christina's fiction and short stories have been published in *Woman's World Magazine* and seven *Chicken Soup for the Soul* books, and you can find her clean romances under the pen name, Lucy McConnell.

To contact Christina, visit her blog: CHRISTINADYMOCK.WORDPRESS.COM